LOOK IT UP

Now in a fully revised edition

Photo Credits: Australian News and Information Bureau; British Tourist Authority; J. Allan Cash; Jesse Davis; Douglas Dickins F.R.P.S.; Featurepix; Henry Grant; Robert Harding Associates; K.I.P.P.A.; Meulenhoff Educatief; Montana Chamber of Commerce; Picturepoint; G.R. Roberts; SATOUR; Spectrum Colour Library; Swiss National Tourist Office; Robert Updegraff; Wiener Sängerknaben; Thomas A. Wilkie Co. Ltd.; ZEFA.

Front cover: Camerapix Hutchison Library.

Illustrators: Fred Anderson; Geoffrey Burns; Richard Eastland; Philip Emms; Dan Escott; John Fraser; Elizabeth Graham-Yool; Ron Haywood; Richard Hook; Eric Jewell; Ben Manchipp; Angus McBride; David Palmer; Mike Roffe: John Sibbick.

Acknowledgements: The Centre for Alternative Technology, Machynlleth, Wales.

First edition © Macmillan Publishers Limited, 1979
Reprinted in 1981, 1982, 1983 and 1984
Second edition © Macmillan Publishers Limited, 1985

Chief Educational Adviser

Lynda Snowdon

Teacher Advisory Panel

Helen Craddock, John Enticknap, Arthur Razzell

Editorial Board

Jan Burgess, Rosemary Canter, Philip M. Clark, Beatrice Phillpotts, Sue Seddon, Philip Steele

Picture Researchers

Caroline Adams, Anne Marie Ehrlich, Gayle Hayter, Ethel Hurwicz, Pat Hodgson, Stella Martin, Frances Middlestorb

Designer

Keith Faulkner

Contributors and consultants

John E. Allen, Neil Ardley, Sue Becklake, Robert Burton, Barry Cox, Jacqueline Dineen, David J. Fletcher, Plantagenet Somerset Fry, Bill Gunston, Robin Kerrod, Mark Lambert, Anne Millard, Kaye Orten, Ian Ridpath, Peter Stephens, Nigel Swann, Aubrey Tulley, Tom Williamson, Thomas Wright

Published by Macmillan Children's Books
a division of Macmillan Publishers Limited
4 Little Essex Street, London WC2R 3LF
Associated companies throughout the world

ISBN 0 333 39720 7 (volume 2)
ISBN 0 333 39568 9 (complete set)

Printed in Hong Kong

People and Customs

Second Edition
LOOK IT UP

Contents

WHERE PEOPLE LIVE

Many people live in cities and towns. There are lots of big offices and factories there where people can work. The outskirts of a city or town are called suburbs.

Some people live in villages out in the country. There are only a few houses and shops in villages. People may work on farms around the village. Some may travel to nearby towns and cities to work.

Villages

In very old villages, the way of life may not have changed very much for many years. Houses are often built from materials found near by. Wood or different types of stone are used a lot. In this village in India the houses have thatched roofs made from dried grass and other plants. The walls are made of stones which are stuck together with mud.

a village in India

In small villages people get to know each other easily and are very friendly. In hot places, like this village in Zambia, children can play together outside all day.

In this village on a Greek island the streets are too narrow for cars. Instead the people use donkeys to carry their goods.

This pretty village is in Austria. The people keep their houses smart and clean. Flowers grow in boxes in the village square.

Towns and cities

Thousands of people live in large cities like this one. The city provides all the things they need. As well as offices, shops and schools, there are parks and cinemas.

In a city there are many different kinds of transport. Some people travel around in cars. Others take the underground railway or a bus.

Homes around the world

Houses in each country can be made with a lot of different materials. A country also often has its own style of houses. This means that the houses look a bit like each other. They do not look like the houses in other countries.

The houses may suit the climate of the country. The house on the right is in the United States. It has a covered porch called a veranda.

These old houses are in Amsterdam in Holland. There are houses of this kind all along the canals of Amsterdam. As you can see they are tall and narrow. This means that more people can live in the city. They also have attractive tops which are called gables.

In Australia the houses are sometimes built on stilts which raise them off the ground. The cool air blows underneath them on hot days.

This house in the picture above is in the south of Spain.

In Spain most of the houses are painted in pale colours. Shutters are pulled down over the windows during the day. This keeps the rooms cool inside. The small balconies are a good place to grow pot plants.

In some countries there is a lot of rain. In these places houses are also built on stilts to protect them from floods.

Flats and playgrounds

Blocks of flats provide homes for lots of people. They take up less space on the ground than houses. The blocks of flats in the picture on the left are in Singapore. The people do not have gardens so they hang their washing out of the windows to dry.

The huge block of flats below is in Australia but it is like many other blocks around the world. In front of it there is a large open space. The children who live in the flats use it as a park and playground.

Some children who live in flats have their own playground outside. These children live in a block of flats in Mexico City.

Old houses are often too big for one family. Sometimes they are divided into several flats. Each flat may take up one floor of the house.

How a house works

A house is used for more than shelter. People eat, sleep, work, relax and entertain friends in their houses. Most houses have several rooms. Electricity provides light and power to make the rooms more comfortable. It comes to the house through thick wires called cables.

The postman delivers letters and the refuse collector takes away the rubbish.

electric wiring

electric socket

rubbish

14

Fresh water comes through pipes
laid underground. Waste water
goes down the drains. Gas for
heating and cooking is also
connected through pipes.

hot
water
tank

water pipes

electricity cables

fresh water

waste water

drains

Homes you can move

Most homes cannot be moved around. If a family wants to live somewhere else, they have to find a new home. There are some kinds of homes that can be moved, such as boats, caravans, and tents.
Their owners may like to travel to find work in different places, or use them on holiday.

These people live in a refugee camp in Cyprus. War has made them homeless, and now they have to live in tents.

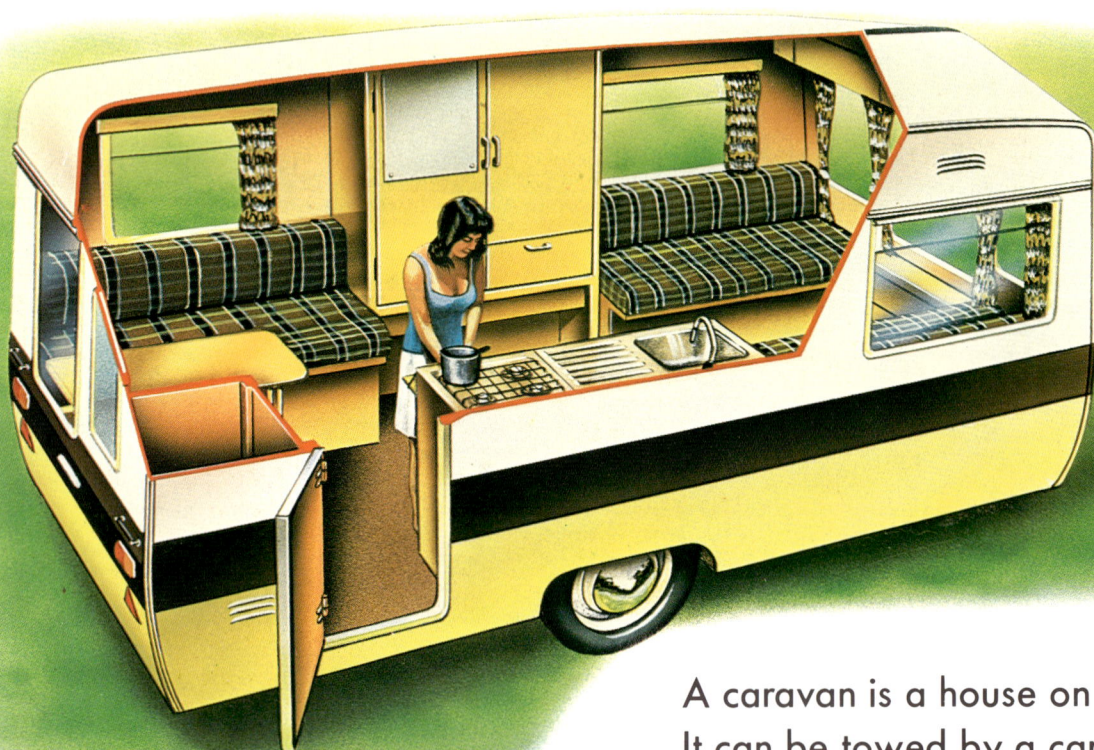

A caravan is a house on wheels. It can be towed by a car. Everything is in a small space, but it is possible to cook, wash, sleep, eat, and sit around inside.

Some cities are too small for everyone to live in. In these cities people may live on houseboats.

These houseboats are crowded together in a harbour in Hong Kong. Thousands of people live on these boats. They use them as fishing boats in the daytime but they eat and sleep on them as well.

These houses are on the island of Madeira. They are painted in bright colours and have thatched roofs which go right down to the ground.

Unusual homes

When you imagine a house, you probably think of the kind of house that you live in. The houses in one country are often the same kind of shape. The buildings look like each other. But there are some buildings that are completely different from the others. Houses in other countries look different too. Which of the houses on this page would you like to live in?

This is not really a house at all. It is a windmill which is not used any more. A family has moved into it and made it into a home.

This strange, tall house is in Suffolk. It was specially built in this way. It is called "The House in the Clouds".

The mud huts in the picture on the left are in the Sudan in Africa. The mud dries and hardens in the sun. Then a straw roof is added.

Homes of the future

We live in houses which need electricity, water, coal or gas to make things work. These all cost a lot of money. Some people have tried building homes which make their own power and heat. Homes like these will probably be common in the future.

This home of the future has a very large roof. It collects rainwater for storage and has solar panels. The panels use the heat of the sun to provide hot water and warmth. A windmill is used to generate electricity, and waste matter is turned into methane gas.

solar-heated swimming pool

windmill generates electricity

solar panels

solar panels

insulated water tank

bathroom

bedroom

conservatory

kitchen

living room

rainwater tank

electric car recharging batteries

accumulator

gutter to collect rainwater

gas cylinder

tank turns waste matter into methane gas

GOING TO SCHOOL

Babies begin to learn as soon as they are born. They soon know their own parents and their brothers and sisters. They hear people talking and begin to use their voices to try to answer. Babies soon learn to sit up, and then to crawl and walk.

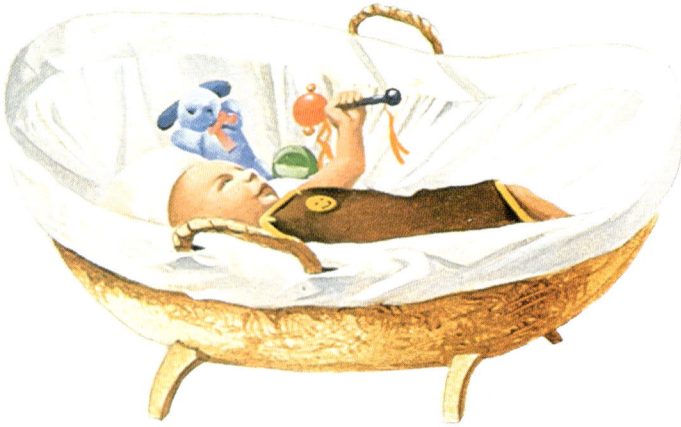

As babies grow into children, they learn from their families and friends. They like to play games. They learn how to use their bodies as they play, so that eyes, hands, arms and legs work together. Mothers and fathers enjoy playing with their children.

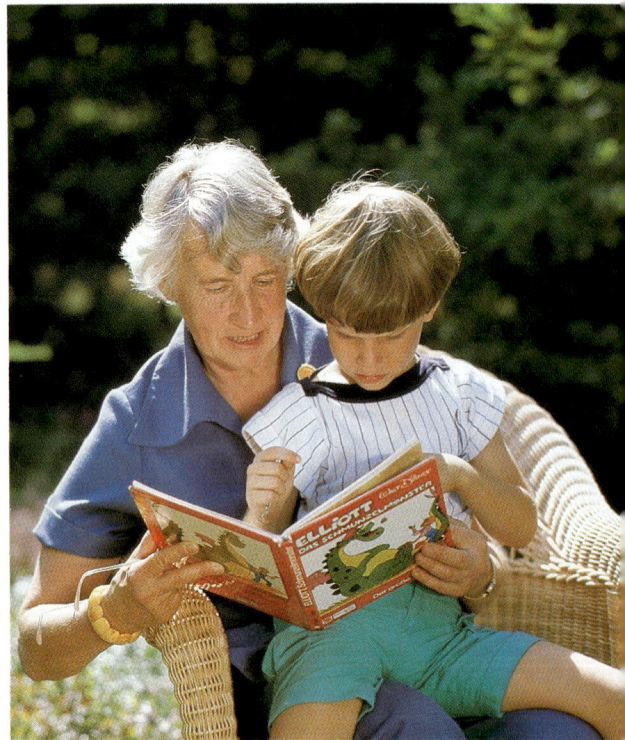

As children grow bigger they learn how to talk. They do this by listening to the people around them, and copying them. As people talk or read stories to them, they learn the words. Children can soon say what they are thinking and ask questions for themselves.

A young child may go to a nursery school or a playgroup. There children play with each other and learn how to make things. They get used to being with different people. The children enjoy making pictures with their new friends.

Primary schools

After nursery school or playgroup, children go to primary school. Here, they learn to read and write, and to use numbers. They paint and play music, and work at crafts.

Once they can read they start to use books to find out the answers to their questions.

At this school in China, the children are learning to use a microscope. You look through a microscope to see things bigger.

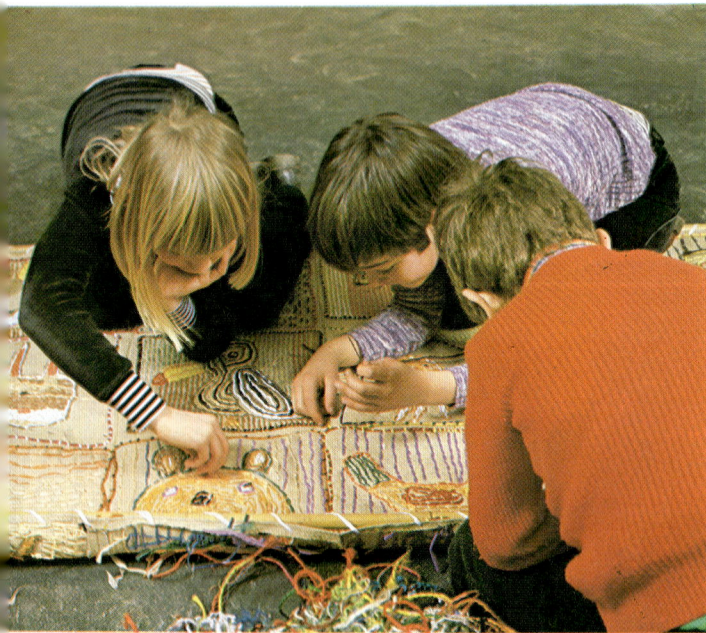

It is fun to make things with different materials. These children are using coloured wools to weave a pretty pattern.

Children may also be given projects to do. They work with other children to make things and find out things for themselves.

The children shown below are working together to build a dragon as part of a project.

There is no building at this school in Nepal. The children sit outside for their lessons.

The children in the school orchestra are good at music. Some of them may become musicians later on.

Secondary schools

After primary school, children go to secondary school. While they are there they will probably find that they like some subjects better than others. This may help them to decide what sort of job they would like to do when they leave school.

Chemistry is taught in a laboratory. A laboratory is a special room for learning about science. Most secondary schools have a laboratory. Here, the pupils can study how different chemicals mix together, like the boy in this picture is doing.

At school everyone learns the usual subjects like history, geography and arithmetic. You can also learn to make things and paint pictures. This girl is learning to paint at a school in Hong Kong. These are some of the pictures which she and her friends have painted.

The children at the bottom are studying metalwork. They are learning how to make things out of metal.

The picture above shows a Chinese girl at school. She is studying calligraphy. Calligraphy means beautiful handwriting. In China there are thousands of letters in the alphabet. They are all different shapes, so there are a lot to learn. Handwriting is a very important subject in China. It is more like painting than writing.

Special schools

Some children go to special schools. There are schools for children who are very good at music or dancing, for example. The picture on the left shows the famous Vienna Boys' Choir. Only very good singers are allowed to join this choir.

Children who are handicapped may also go to special schools.
The children in the big picture are deaf. They have special machines to help them learn more easily.

Children at special schools for music and dancing have lessons in ordinary subjects like other children.

These children are at a ballet school in Russia. In the picture above they are having a geography lesson. On the desk is a globe. A globe shows all the countries in the world.

They also have to work very hard at their ballet classes. They practise their ballet exercises at the bar, like the girl in the picture on the left. A bar teaches you to stand correctly.

FOOD

Some of our food comes from animals. Early man used to hunt animals for food. Then he learnt to keep certain animals in fields so that he did not have to hunt for them.

We also eat fish and other creatures that live in water. Fishermen go out to sea and catch them with nets. Fish farmers have lakes or ponds where they keep fish for eating.

Some people do not eat meat.
They eat food mainly from plants,
such as vegetables, fruit, cereals,
and nuts. There are lots of different
plant foods to choose from.

Wheat and rice are two important
cereals. Farmers grow them in fields
and harvest them every year.
In some countries cereals like rice
are the main supply of food.

Different kinds of food

Meat is sometimes processed to make other foods, such as sausages, bacon and ham. These all come from the pig. Milk, cheese and butter all come from animals.

You can buy whole, fresh fish at the fishmonger. Fish can also be frozen to keep it fresh longer. Some fish is smoked to keep it fresh. Some fish, like sardines, are sold in cans.

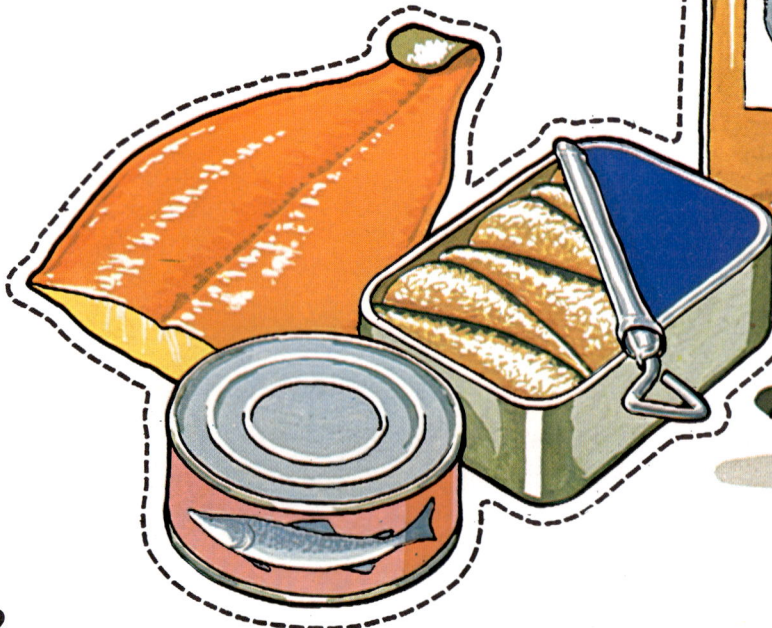

Drinks such as tea, coffee, and wine are made from plants. Herbs and spices come from plants too. Fruit is used to make jam and to flavour jellies and drinks.

The most important cereal product is flour. People make foods like bread, cakes and pasta with flour. Breakfast foods, beer and whisky are also made with cereals.

Where does food come from?

We do not buy our food straight from the farmer or fisherman. We buy it from shops. How does it get to the shops? The farmer sends the food to a central market.

The cow is milked at the farm and the milk is sent to the dairy.

The fish are caught in nets and taken back to the ports.

Fruit and vegetables are picked when they are ripe.

At harvest time the corn is cut with a combine harvester.

The fish that is caught goes from the port to a fish market. Fruit and vegetables are sent to special markets as well. Shopkeepers go to these markets to choose food for their shops. Corn is sent to a mill. It is ground to make flour for bread and other food.

Small food shops sell some of the foods you need.

In a big supermarket you can buy all types of food.

In some towns there are street markets where you can buy food.

Eating and drinking

Not all food plants can be grown in all countries. People used to eat just the food which grew in their own country. Now food is sold by one country to another. Many people enjoy food from foreign countries.

Countries have their own customs for eating and drinking too. In Japan tea is a favourite drink. The Japanese tea party is a formal occasion. The lady on the left is preparing tea.

Rice grows in Eastern countries and a lot of it is eaten there. This man is cooking simple rice dishes in a city street in India. The rice is made with nuts and raisins in it.

A picnic is usually eaten out of doors and away from home. If you go away for the day your mother may pack a picnic meal to take with you.

These two girls from Italy are eating pasta. Pasta is made in Italy in many different shapes and sizes. Spaghetti is a favourite kind. It is difficult to eat because it is very long.

In some towns there are foodstalls on the roadside. You can buy food there which is ready to eat. This is a herring stall in a Dutch town.

CLOTHES

Leather comes from the skins of animals such as cattle or pigs. Because it is strong, it is used to make tough clothes and boots, shoes and handbags.

Cotton comes from the cotton plant. The fibres are spun and then woven into cloth. Cotton clothes are light and cool. They are comfortable to wear in hot weather.

Wool comes from sheep. Every spring their coats are cut short and the wool is spun into long lengths. It is knitted into warm clothes like jumpers, socks and gloves.

Nowadays, cloth can be made from chemicals. These 'man-made' cloths may not need ironing. They are often lighter than other types of cloth but they are also very warm.

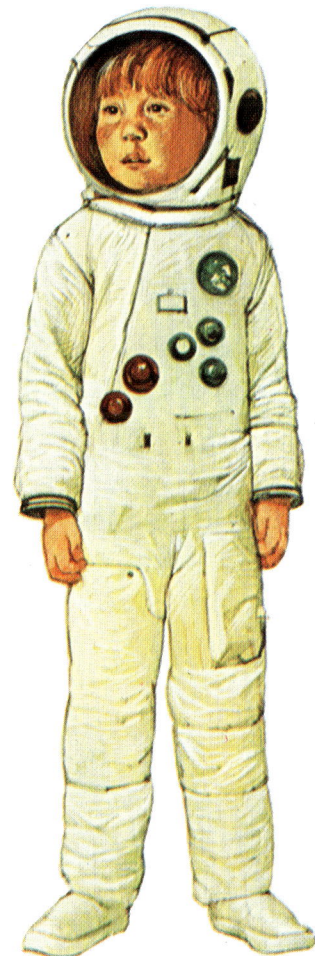

Clothes around the world

People from different parts of the world wear different clothes. This is often because of the climate. Some countries have their own traditional costumes.

The Japanese lady below is wearing a 'kimono'. This is the traditional costume of Japan.

These people live in the mountains in Turkey. It is very cold up there so they need to wear warm clothes. The women cover their heads with thick woollen shawls.

The children in the picture below
live in Lapland near the North Pole.
They are wearing the traditional
costumes of the Lapps. The clothes
have lots of gay trimmings.

Arab people live in hot countries in
Asia and Africa. They wear long
loose robes to keep off the sun.

Arabs also wear a head-dress which
they can wrap around their faces.
This protects them from sandstorms
in the desert.

Uniforms

People wear uniforms for certain jobs. You may have to wear a uniform at school. A uniform helps people to recognize what job you do. It shows that you belong to a special group. Some people are very proud of the uniforms they wear. Their dress is very smart, with brass buttons and badges. Other uniforms are more practical. They are worn every day for work.

nurse
Great Britain

colonel-in-charge
Spanish riding school

Girl guides and boy scouts wear different uniforms in different countries. When they pass special tests, they can wear extra badges on their shirts. The armed forces of each country wear different uniforms too.

girl guide
Great Britain

42

naval officer
USA

In a hospital emergency, it is important to know who is a nurse. The nurses wear clean, simple uniforms. Airline crews always wear smart outfits. In some countries the stewardesses wear pretty saris.

motorcycle
patrolman USA

air hostess
Singapore

If you lose your way in the street you might want to ask someone the way. A policeman would be a good person to ask. You would know him by his uniform. Motor cycle police wear different clothes. They have boots and crash helmets.

Jewellery and decoration

These women live in Nepal.
They cover their arms with bangles.
Can you see their big earrings?
Some of them wear nose rings too.

Ornaments and jewellery are used for decoration. In some countries people wear them in traditional ways. This African woman and her child wear special coloured bands which you would not see in other parts of the world.

Young people all over the world are interested in fashion. Some like to wear extraordinary clothes and jewellery. Others prefer jeans and casual clothes.

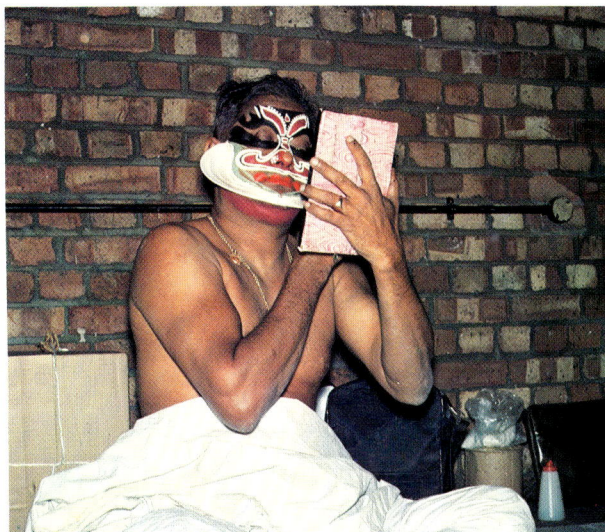

Paint has been used as body decoration for a very long time. Indonesian dancers like this man cover their whole bodies with paint.

Thailand is famous for its dancing. The dancers wear beautiful costumes and tall hats. These are covered with patterns made of jewels.

RELIGION

Many people in the world believe in God, or in a number of different gods. The various beliefs and ways of worship are called religions.

Christianity

Christians follow the teachings of Jesus Christ. They worship God in a church, like this one in Greece. The priest on the left is leading a Roman Catholic service.

Judaism

Judaism is the religion of people known as Jews. They believe in one God alone and they worship in a synagogue. They say their prayers in Hebrew. Their religious leaders are called rabbis. Judaism is one of the oldest religions in the world.

The Wailing Wall in Jerusalem shown below is the most holy place for Jews. Many of them go to visit and pray there.

Hinduism

Hinduism is a religion of India. This Hindu priest sits calmly in a temple in India. Hindus believe that we have many lives. We must learn to lead a better life each time.

Hindus worship many gods and goddesses in temples and at home. They build statues of them, like this one below.

Islam

Islam is the religion of people called Muslims. They follow the teachings of Muhammed who was born in Mecca in AD 570.

Muslims worship their God, Allah, in a mosque like this one which is in Turkey. A crier calls them to prayer from the tower. Muslims take their shoes off to worship.

Buddhism

Most Buddhists live in southern Asia. They follow the teachings of Buddha, who lived in India 2,500 years ago. Buddhists do not worship any god. People go to worship in temples, like this one in Thailand.

There are also monasteries where monks can study the religion. Buddhist monks wear yellow robes.

Shinto

The religion of Japan is called Shinto. It is a very old religion.

People believe in many gods and spirits. They worship them in their homes and at shrines. They make little gifts to the gods and hope to get their blessing. Shinto festivals are celebrated with processions and ceremonies.

CUSTOMS AROUND THE WORLD

People everywhere have different days which are important to them. Sometimes they remember a famous event every year, often on the same date. Other ceremonies, such as weddings, are performed only once. There are some dates which mean something to whole countries. For really big celebrations people sometimes have fireworks.

Birthday celebrations

Your birthday is probably your most important celebration because it is a special day for you. It marks the day you were born. You may invite friends to a party on that day. In some countries everyone with the same name celebrates on one day.

Coming of age

'Coming of age' is a particularly important birthday celebration.

It is the time when a young person has reached the age of an adult. At this coming of age ceremony in Africa, people dance and wear masks.

The custom called Bar Mitzvah (shown on the right) is a Jewish celebration for a boy's thirteenth birthday.

Wedding ceremonies

Although all weddings are ceremonies to marry two people, they are not always the same. What happens at a wedding depends on the religion or customs of the country the people come from.

The bride at this Muslim wedding in India receives money from the guests. The picture on the right shows people in traditional costume at a wedding in Mexico.

A wedding may be a religious ceremony, in a church. A lot of weddings do not take place in a church, and these do not have any religious customs. All weddings mark the bond between the two people. In a Christian wedding, the groom gives the bride a ring. In the Japanese wedding shown here, the couple sip cups of wine.

This picture of a village wedding shows a Swedish custom. A band leads a procession of the people taking part.

Funerals

A funeral is a religious ceremony which is held when someone dies.

People are usually buried in a holy place like a churchyard. In some countries the family and friends wear black at a funeral to show their sadness. Other funerals are bright parades. This brightly painted box is a Chinese coffin. At a grave in Indonesia, statues of the dead person's ancestors watch over the burial place.

This gay procession in Bali,
Indonesia, is also a funeral. The
coffin is put inside the statue of a
bull and carried through the streets.

Christmas

At Christmas Christians all over the world celebrate the birth of Jesus Christ. They give each other presents and decorate a tree.

Children hang up stockings and St Nicholas, the patron saint of children, fills them with presents. In the Netherlands he has young helpers dressed as black boys.

There are some strange customs which people have followed for many years at Christmas time and New Year. Look at the funny things which these people are doing. Do you follow any of these customs?

New Year

The beginning of each New Year is celebrated in most countries.

On New Year's Eve some people go to church. Others invite friends round to their homes. When the clock strikes midnight they all welcome the New Year together. The Chinese New Year begins on a different date.

Unusual customs

Most countries have their own customs which are not seen anywhere else. Many of these ceremonies have been performed for a long time.

This African man is walking on stilts. He is taking part in a ceremony for chasing away evil spirits.

Every year on December 6th, people in Switzerland dress up in big hats with candles inside, as you can see in the picture below.

The picture on the left shows some children doing maypole dancing. Maypole dancing is an old custom which you can still see in country parts of Britain. As the people dance around the maypole, they hold coloured ribbons. The ribbons wind around the pole in a pattern.

Carnivals happen all over the world. People dress up and parade through the streets. There are bands playing music, and people dance. Sometimes whole towns join in. The costumes are bright and strange, like this one from Trinidad.

DID YOU KNOW?

Not many people live to be 100. We know of at least one person who lived to be 113.

One of the cleverest children who ever lived was called Wolfgang Mozart. He lived in Austria about 200 years ago. He wrote his first symphony when he was only five.

The heaviest man ever known lived in America. He weighed 171 kilos when he was only 10. When he was grown up he weighed 485 kilos. His waist measured about 3 metres.

Imagine how big his clothes must have been. How many people do you think could get into a pair of his trousers?

INDEX